the living Ocean

Polar Oceans

Bobbie Kalman & Molly Aloian

🌳 Crabtree Publishing Company

www.crabtreebooks.com

the Living Ocean

Created by Bobbie Kalman

Dedicated by Margaret Amy Reiach
For Tray Salter
Whose warm Southern ways have made this snowbird smile

Editor-in-Chief
Bobbie Kalman

Writing team
Bobbie Kalman
Molly Aloian

Editorial director
Niki Walker

Editors
Amanda Bishop
Rebecca Sjonger
Kathryn Smithyman

Art director
Robert MacGregor

Design
Margaret Amy Reiach

Production coordinator
Heather Fitzpatrick

Photo research
Laura Hysert

Consultant
Patricia Loesche, Ph.D., Animal Behavior Program,
Department of Psychology, University of Washington

Photographs
Seapics.com: © Michael S. Nolan: pages 10 (bottom), 17 (top);
© Dan Salden: page 11; © Franco Banfi: pages 13, 15, 30;
© Richard Ellis: page 14 (bottom); © John K. B. Ford/Ursus: page 17 (bottom);
© Kevin Schafer: pages 18, 20 (bottom), 21 (top); © Dan Burton: page 28;
© Doc White: page 31 (top)
Tom Stack & Associates: © Mark Newman: page 29 (top)
Other images by Digital Vision, Digital Stock, World Art Inc., and Corbis

Illustrations
Margaret Amy Reiach: pages 11 (zooplankton & phytoplankton), 12 (top),
    22-25 (phytoplankton, clams, snail, herring)
Barbara Bedell: pages 11 (krill & magnifying glasses), 16, 22-25 (krill, orca,
    polar bear, penguin, humpback whale)
Bonna Rouse: pages 12 (bottom), 15, 22-25 (background, starfish, squid,
    octopus, antarctic cod, wandering albatross, Weddell seal), 31
Katherine Kantor: pages 22-24 (arctic tern, arctic cod, ringed seal, walrus,
    leopard seal)
Trevor Morgan: pages 22-23 (harp seal)

Crabtree Publishing Company

www.crabtreebooks.com   1-800-387-7650

PMB 16A	612 Welland Avenue	73 Lime Walk
350 Fifth Avenue	St. Catharines	Headington
Suite 3308	Ontario	Oxford
New York, NY	Canada	OX3 7AD
10118	L2M 5V6	United Kingdom

Cataloging-in-Publication Data
Kalman, Bobbie
   Polar oceans / Bobbie Kalman & Molly Aloian.
      p. cm. — (The Living ocean series)
This book examines the diverse lifeforms that thrive in the extreme
climates of the oceans surrounding the North and South Poles, the
differences between Arctic and Antarctic waters, and the global
consequences of environmental changes.
   ISBN 0-7787-1297-4 (RLB) — ISBN 0-7787-1319-9 (pbk.)
   1. Marine biology—Polar regions—Juvenile literature. [1. Marine
biology—Polar regions. 2. Ocean. 3. Polar regions.] I. Aloian, Molly.
II. Title. III. Series.
QH95.56.K36 2003
   577.7—dc21
                                                          2003004548
                                                          LC

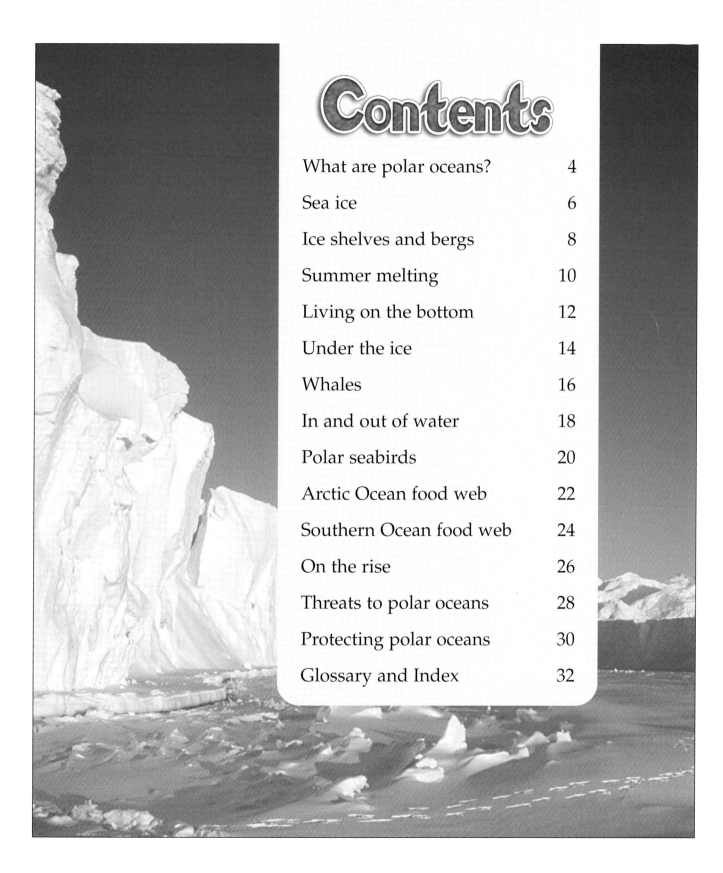

Contents

What are polar oceans?

Oceans cover more than three-quarters of the Earth's surface. An ocean is a huge body of **salt water**. There are five oceans—Atlantic, Pacific, Indian, Arctic, and Southern. The Arctic and Southern Oceans are called **polar** oceans because they are located at the Earth's poles. The Arctic Ocean covers the North Pole. It is bordered by the northern coasts of Greenland, North America, and Asia. The Southern Ocean surrounds the South Pole and Antarctica.

Although all oceans are huge, the polar oceans are not as vast as the others. The Southern Ocean covers about eight million square miles (20.7 million km²), and it reaches depths of up to 23,737 feet (7235 m). The Arctic Ocean covers about five million square miles (12.9 million km²) and, in most places, is about 4,900 feet (1500 m) deep. By comparison, the largest ocean—the Pacific—covers an area twenty times as large as the Arctic Ocean and is almost three times as deep.

Freezing climate

The poles have the coldest, windiest, and driest **climates** on Earth, making polar ocean waters very cold. The average temperature of the Arctic Ocean is between 28° F (-2° C) and 33° F (0.6° C). The Southern Ocean is slightly warmer—between 28° F (-2° C) and 50° F (10° C).

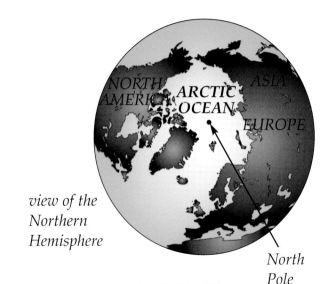

view of the Northern Hemisphere

North Pole

Icy oceans

The temperatures at the poles are so cold that the surfaces of the polar oceans freeze into floating patches of **sea ice**. Sea ice becomes larger and thicker during winter and melts and shrinks in summer. There is always some ice, however. A massive sheet of sea ice floats year-round on the center of the Arctic Ocean. Although most of the Southern Ocean's sea ice melts in summer, blocks of sea ice up to ten feet (3 m) thick and 932 miles (1500 km) wide always extend from the coast of the Southern Ocean.

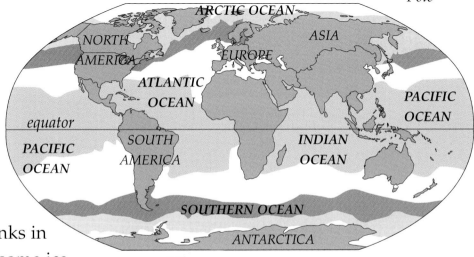

*The **equator** divides the world into the **Northern Hemisphere** and the **Southern Hemisphere**. The North and South poles are located in opposite hemispheres.*

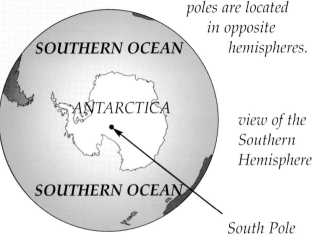

view of the Southern Hemisphere

South Pole

*The polar oceans include many **seas**, such as the Weddell Sea in the Southern Ocean and the Barents Sea in the Arctic Ocean. A sea is a small area of an ocean that is partly or completely surrounded by land.*

Sea ice

Polar oceans are home to many living things. Polar **ecosystems** include plants, animals, and nonliving things such as sand or rocks. Sea ice is an important part of polar ecosystems. The living things in polar oceans depend on sea ice to keep their surroundings cold. The ice blocks the heat from the sun and maintains the cold temperatures of the water. It also provides habitats for many animals, such as the polar bear shown left. Some animals live on the ice, some hunt on it, and others live underneath it.

How sea ice forms

As temperatures grow colder in polar regions, small crystals of ice, called **frazil ice**, form on the surface of the water. When the temperature drops farther, more water freezes against the frazil ice. The layer of ice may become up to three feet (1 m) thick. Eventually, the layers turn into ice **floes**, or large flat sheets of floating ice. When floes freeze together, they form huge sheets of **pack ice**. Pack ice is usually about ten feet (3 m) thick.

Thicker and thicker

In one winter, sea ice can become one to three feet (0.3-1 m) thick. The polar oceans are so cold that not all the ice melts in summer. When sea ice freezes over two or more winters, it may become up to sixteen feet (5 m) thick. This ice is called **multi-year ice**. Both the Southern and Arctic Oceans have multi-year ice floes, although the Arctic Ocean has more of them.

Animals such as seals and penguins rest on sea ice, raise their young on it, and dive off it to hunt in the water below.

Extra-salty water

All oceans are **saline**, or contain salt, but sea ice makes polar oceans even more saline. When salt water freezes, only the water becomes ice. Salt does not freeze. Instead, it remains in the unfrozen water below the ice. As a result, the water has more salt. Because it contains more salt, the water in polar oceans is **denser**, or thicker and heavier, than that found in other oceans. It is much denser than air or fresh water. The denser water is, the more difficult it is to move through it, but objects can float on it more easily. For example, huge chunks of ice float on the polar oceans because the water supports them.

Getting some air

Mammals such as seals and whales breathe air. They must find ways to get through the ice to breathe. Seals and orcas breathe at holes in the ice or in areas without sea ice, as shown above. Seals often chew or scratch the edges of their breathing holes to keep them open. Some whales push against the ice with their backs to lift or smash it.

Ice shelves and bergs

Ice forms on the surfaces of polar oceans, and it also builds up on the land around them. On Antarctica and on the many islands in the Arctic Ocean, ice combines with snow and, in time, forms huge sheets called **glaciers**. Some of these glaciers reach the **coastlines**, or ocean edges, and extend out over the oceans. Water freezes against these sheets to form huge **ice shelves**. Ice shelves often look more like ice cliffs. Some tower more than 3,280 feet (1000 m) above the ocean's surface.

Ice shelves

An ice shelf is a massive sheet of floating ice that is frozen against land on one edge. Ice shelves cover about half of the Antarctic coastline. In the Arctic Ocean, most ice shelves form along the coasts of Greenland and the northeastern parts of Canada. Some ice shelves stretch out more than 450 miles (724 km) over the ocean's surface!

*In Antarctica, huge **colonies**, or groups, of emperor penguins live on ice shelves. The penguins often huddle together to keep warm.*

Breaking off

Ice shelves and glaciers along coasts are battered by waves, wind, and **tides**. The ice often cracks, and giant pieces **calve**, or break off. When these massive chunks float into the ocean, they are called **icebergs**. Most icebergs calve in spring and summer, when warmer temperatures loosen the tightly packed snow and ice. Icebergs are pushed through the polar oceans and seas by **currents** and winds. Icebergs can travel up to twelve miles (19 km) per day.

Huge ice cubes

The size of an iceberg can be deceiving because only a small portion of it shows above the water's surface. Southern Ocean icebergs are massive! They can be more than 60 miles (96 km) long. They are much larger than those found in the Arctic Ocean. The icebergs in the Arctic Ocean are mostly **growlers**. Growlers are about the size of cars. Larger icebergs, called **bergy bits**, are about the size of houses.

*The top of an iceberg is mainly snow and loosely packed ice. The **core**, or center, is densely packed ice. This ice is much heavier than the snow and ice on top, so it sinks below the surface of the water.*

Summer melting

In winter, the sea ice on the Southern Ocean covers more than seven million square miles (18 million km²). On the Arctic Ocean, winter sea ice covers up to five million square miles (13 million km²).

Whales feed in the polar oceans in summer. The Southern Ocean's sea ice shrinks to two million square miles (4 million km²). In the Arctic, sea ice shrinks to less than four million square miles (10 million km²).

When it is summer at the North Pole, it is winter at the South Pole. The poles have opposite seasons because they are in different hemispheres—the sun hits them most directly at different times of the year. Even though the seasons occur at opposite times, they are similar at both poles. Summers are cold and short, and winters are long and freezing cold. During summer, the sun never sets completely, so there is constant daylight. Sunlight melts about half of the sea ice. During winter, however, the sun does not rise completely. New sea ice forms, and older ice becomes thicker.

Open water

In winter, the oceans are almost totally covered with thick, solid ice. In summer, some of the ice melts and cracks. Chunks of ice break apart. Patches of open water, called **polynyas**, appear between the chunks. The polynyas in both the polar oceans are most common in seas and near coastlines. Whales such as belugas often feed on fish and other **prey** in polynyas.

Life in summer

Polar oceans are home to more life in summer than in winter because there is more sunlight and food. During summer, millions of microscopic floating plants called **phytoplankton** grow. Phytoplankton are the only plants found in polar oceans. They grow near the surface because they need sunlight and nutrients to make food. Microscopic animals, called **zooplankton**, feed on the phytoplankton. In summer, the huge amounts of **plankton**—phytoplankton and zooplankton—attract many animals to the oceans to feed.

Thrilled with krill

Tiny shrimplike animals called **krill** are a type of zooplankton that thrive in the polar oceans in summer. Krill feed on phytoplankton near the ocean's surface. Some krill live in the Arctic Ocean, but there are gigantic swarms of krill in the Southern Ocean. Krill is a major source of food for many marine animals, including whales, seals, fish, squids, penguins, and other seabirds. See pages 16-17 and 24 to 27 for more on plankton, krill, and the animals that eat them.

phytoplankton

zooplankton

Humpback whales feed on swarms of krill in polar waters.

Living on the bottom

The coastlines of polar oceans are often covered with ice. Under the ice, the ocean floor is dark and sandy. An amazing variety of living things can be found on the sandy bottoms, including colorful soft corals, sea urchins, anemones, and sponges.

Some living things, including clams, worms, snails, and crabs, bury themselves in the sand. Others, such as sea spiders, brittle stars, and sea stars, move along the ocean floor. Some bottom dwellers, including anemones, burrow in the sand to hide from predators. Others hide in the cracks found in rocks.

For much of the year, the sandy bottoms of polar oceans are under the shadows of thick layers of ice.

Slow to grow

Animals that live in polar oceans often go without food for much of the year. With little food energy, the animals cannot grow much. As a result, polar species grow slower than animals of the same species that live in warmer waters. Because polar animals grow slowly, they often live longer.

Taking it easy

Animals use energy to breathe, feed, and move. With little food available, polar bottom dwellers must save as much of their energy as they can. They cannot afford to use most of it searching for food. Some save energy by moving very slowly. Many do not move at all! Some animals grab tiny bits of food as the food floats past. Others **filter**, or strain, food from the water. Soft corals sift through the sand for dead plankton that drift down from the ocean's surface.

Making food last

Polar bottom dwellers **digest**, or break down, their food more slowly than do bottom dwellers in warm waters. Digesting their food slowly gives them energy for longer periods of time. They do not use up energy as quickly as warm-water animals do, so they can go longer without food.

Anemones use their many long tentacles to catch prey such as sea stars, sea urchins, and even huge sea jellies.

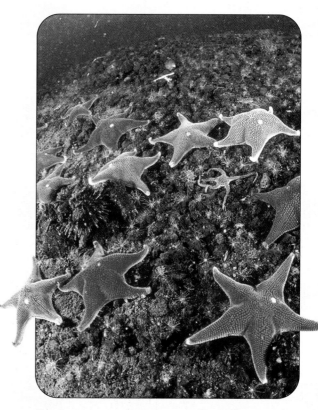

Sea stars use their sense of smell to locate prey such as clams, mussels, and scallops.

13

Under the ice

Like bottom dwellers, animals swimming beneath the ice digest their food slowly to conserve energy.

Octopuses, squids, sea jellies, and fish are among the polar animals that live beneath the sea ice. Some spend time resting or hiding on the ocean floor, but they also swim in search of food. Each animal is well suited to surviving in the dark, cold waters. The animals are also important prey for many larger **predators**, including seabirds, whales, and seals.

Underwater homes

Octopuses live under rocks or in crevices where they can hide from predators. Most swim at night, hunting for fish, snails, scallops, and other prey. Giant squid live in deeper waters. Some fish, including plaice and halibut, swim along the bottom in shallow areas of the oceans. Others, such as cod, hide in the cracks and crevices of sea ice or icebergs.

Sperm whales hunt giant squids in deep waters.

14

Antifreeze fish

There are about 200 **species**, or types, of fish in the Southern Ocean, including flounder, herring, icefish, and lantern fish. The Arctic Ocean is home to more than 70 species of fish, including char, cod, halibut, and salmon. Polar fish have many adaptations that help them live and hunt in the freezing waters. Some species, such as cod and sculpin, have substances in their blood that keep it from freezing. Other fish species lack red blood cells, which most animals need to carry oxygen throughout their bodies. Polar waters are so rich in oxygen, however, that the fish absorb the oxygen directly into their bodies. They do not need red blood cells to carry oxygen.

The blood of this striped rock cod does not freeze, even in extremely cold temperatures.

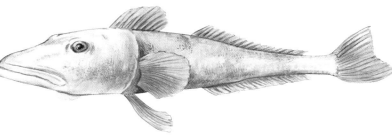

*Fish without red blood cells are **translucent**—you can see light through their bodies.*

Hiding with the light

Some squid species are **bioluminescent**, or have special organs that produce light. These light organs help squids hide from predators and prey. The light allows them to blend in with the glittering sunlight that filters through the water. From below, predators and prey cannot see a squid against the brightly lit surface above. When there is little sunlight in the water, a squid's organs produce only a small amount of light. When there is plenty of sunlight, the squid's organs produce more light.

Whales

Whales are well suited to the icy waters of the Southern and Arctic Oceans, even though few of them live at the poles year-round. Like most marine mammals, whales have a thick layer of fat under their skin, called **blubber**, which keeps them warm in icy waters.

A sperm whale is a toothed whale.

A right whale is a baleen whale.

Baleen whales have plates of baleen in their mouths to filter krill and other small prey from the water. Baleen whales such as blue whales, Minke whales, and humpback whales, shown above, travel to the polar oceans in summer to feed on swarms of krill. **Toothed whales** have sharp teeth for grabbing and biting prey. These whales include orcas, beluga whales, and sperm whales. They hunt fish, squids, penguins, and seals in the polar oceans. Most toothed whales travel in groups called **pods**, or schools.

Leaving the cold behind

Many whales feed on krill and plankton in the polar oceans in summer. Others swim there to hunt the squids, fish, and larger prey that feed on krill. By early autumn, however, polar temperatures drop, and the krill and other plankton populations begin to die off. Solid ice begins to form along the shorelines. When this ice starts to form, most of the whales leave the polar oceans and swim to warmer waters, where they mate and give birth. Humpback whales, blue whales, and fin whales travel north from the Southern Ocean in winter. A few beluga whales and narwhals also **migrate** south from the Arctic Ocean to warmer waters.

The beluga whales above are swimming in a pod. They stay close together for protection against predators, and they hunt as a group.

Living year-round

Although most whales are found in the polar oceans only in summer, a few species stay year-round in the icy Arctic Ocean. They include beluga whales and narwhals. Polynyas and smaller cracks in the ice, called **leads**, provide the open areas that these whales need for breathing. Scientists are still trying to find out if any whales live in the Southern Ocean all year.

Narwhals are one of two types of whales that live year-round in the Arctic Ocean. They feed on fish, squids, and crustaceans.

In and out of water

Many polar animals spend only part of their time underwater. They hunt in the oceans but **haul out**, or heave themselves, onto ice or land to rest or have babies. Most animals that haul out are marine mammals such as walruses, seals, and polar bears. Different species of these animals live in the Arctic and Southern Oceans. For example, harp seals and hooded seals live in the Arctic Ocean, whereas fur seals and Weddell seals live in the Southern Ocean. Walruses and polar bears live only in and around the Arctic Ocean.

Staying warm

Mammals are **warm-blooded**, which means their bodies stay the same temperature no matter how warm or cold their surroundings are. Polar mammals have a thick layer of blubber to keep their body heat from escaping. Many also have muscles that become very warm when they swim. Their bodies use this heat to stay warm in and out of the water.

The mothers of harp seal pups have milk that is rich in fat, which helps the pups gain weight and develop blubber quickly.

18

Keeping out the cold

Some polar mammals, including polar bears and fur seals, have thick coats of fur that help keep cold air and water away from their bodies. Their coats are made up of two layers. A thick, soft layer of short **underfur** traps heat against their skin. Long **guard hairs** keep cold water away from the underfur and skin when the animals swim. Guard hairs dry quickly in the air.

Seals have a mirror-like layer at the back of their eyes, which helps them see in the dark, ice-covered parts of the oceans.

Walruses are huge mammals! They can weigh up to 1,985 pounds (900 kg). Their blubber is up to four inches (10 cm) thick.

On the ice

Polar bears are equally well suited to running on ice and swimming in the oceans. They have wide, flat paws to help them move easily over fresh snow and slippery ice, as well as small **webs**, or flaps of skin, between their toes to help them swim. Their fur is oily and waterproof. With a few shakes, the bears can remove most of the water from their fur after swimming. Their skin is black, a color that absorbs the sun's heat, to help keep the bears warm. A layer of blubber up to five inches (13 cm) thick insulates the bears from the cold wind and water.

Polar seabirds

Arctic terns travel farther than any bird. They spend the summer in the Arctic and fly to the Southern Ocean when winter arrives. Their journey is more than 21,750 miles (35 000 km)!

Like most seabirds, these cormorants nest in large colonies on cliffs above the polar oceans.

The only birds that live year-round in the polar oceans are a few species of penguins. They cannot fly, so they spend much of their time swimming in the oceans. Most other seabirds, including albatrosses, petrels, skuas, fulmars, gulls, auks, sheathbills, cormorants, puffins, and terns spend only part of the year in polar areas. These birds fly over the polar oceans, dive down to hunt, and return to shore to nest and rest.

Just visiting

In the spring, huge colonies of seabirds nest near the polar oceans. They raise their chicks during the short summer, when there is plenty of food in the water. Before winter arrives, most seabirds migrate with their young to the warmer waters in the Atlantic and Pacific Oceans. In winter, there is more prey in the warmer oceans than there is in polar waters.

Diving for dinner

Seabirds feed on a variety of prey. Many birds, including petrels and terns, fly above the ocean and dive down to snatch fish, squids, and other prey near the surface. Some, such as kittiwakes and fulmars, float on the ocean's surface, where they feed on krill. A few birds, including penguins, auks, and cormorants, dive deep underwater to chase fish, squids, and other prey.

This huge flock of northern fulmars is feeding on prey at the ocean's surface.

"Flying" underwater

Penguins are well suited to living in freezing waters. They have waterproof feathers that overlap so tightly that their skin never gets wet. Under these feathers, penguins have a layer of soft, downy feathers that holds warm air against their skin. Penguins also have a thick layer of blubber to keep in their body heat. They are able to dive deep in search of prey, and some species can hold their breath for more than ten minutes. Penguins use their stiff wings to "fly" underwater, and they steer with their webbed feet.

*Penguins have **streamlined**, or sleekly shaped, bodies that help them swim quickly and easily.*

Arctic Ocean food web

All living things need energy from food to survive. Plants are the only living things that can make their own food using the sun's energy. Some animals get food energy by eating plants. Others get energy by eating plant-eaters. In a **food chain**, energy moves from one creature to the next. The yellow arrows below show how energy moves through food chains.

Predators such as orcas and polar bears are at the **apex**, or top, of many Arctic Ocean food chains. When predators eat animals from other food chains, the food chains connect to form a **food web**.

Arctic tern

Short chains

Fewer species of animals live in polar oceans than in warmer oceans. For example, six seal species live in the Arctic Ocean, but up to twenty seal species live in warmer waters. Since there are fewer species, Arctic animals have fewer food choices. Each species relies on a few food sources, which makes Arctic Ocean food chains much shorter than the food chains in other oceans.

Arctic cod

krill

orca

phytoplankton

harp seal

clams

snail

It all depends on plankton!

This food web is largest in summer, when the sun melts patches of sea ice and phytoplankton can grow. Plankton is at the beginning of each Arctic Ocean food chain, which makes this food source very important.

Every animal relies on phytoplankton for survival, whether it eats plankton or not. For example, Arctic cod feed on phytoplankton and, in turn, become food for many other animals, including harp seals, ringed seals, and seabirds. Polar bears hunt these animals, so they, too, rely on the plankton indirectly.

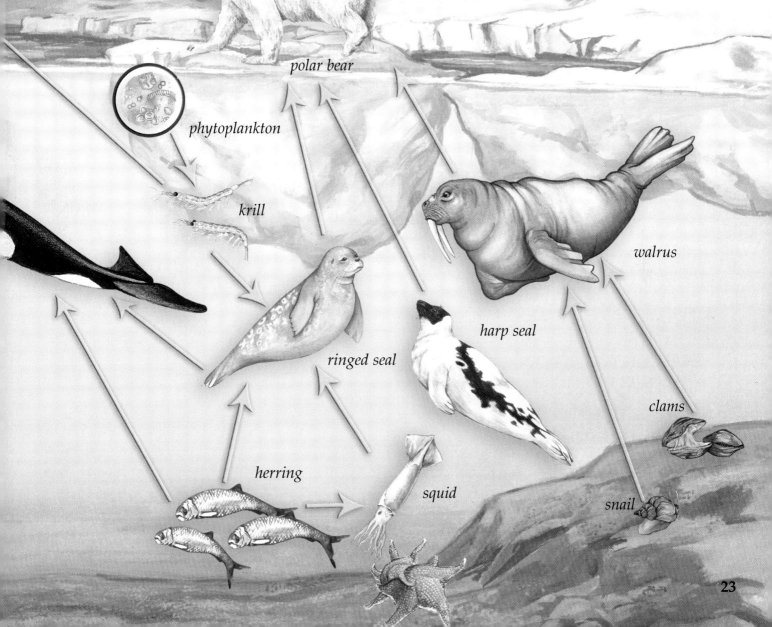

polar bear

phytoplankton

krill

walrus

harp seal

ringed seal

clams

herring

squid

snail

23

Southern Ocean food web

The Southern Ocean is richer in life than the Arctic Ocean is, but its food chains are still short. As in the Arctic Ocean, there are only a few species of animals, so each species relies on a limited number of food sources. Krill, fish, squids, and penguins are eaten by seals and whales.

wandering albatross

phytoplankton

krill

penguin

squid

octopus

Antarctic cod

leopard seal

snail

Feeding on krill

The Southern Ocean is full of life in spring and summer. Huge swarms of krill feed on the phytoplankton that grow at the ocean's surface. Krill is part of almost every food chain. Whales, seals, squids, fish, and seabirds all feed on krill.

Apex predators in the Southern Ocean include orcas and leopard seals. Unlike the polar bears of the Arctic Ocean, these animals are a threat to their prey only when they are underwater. The seals and penguins they hunt often haul out onto the sea ice, where they are safe.

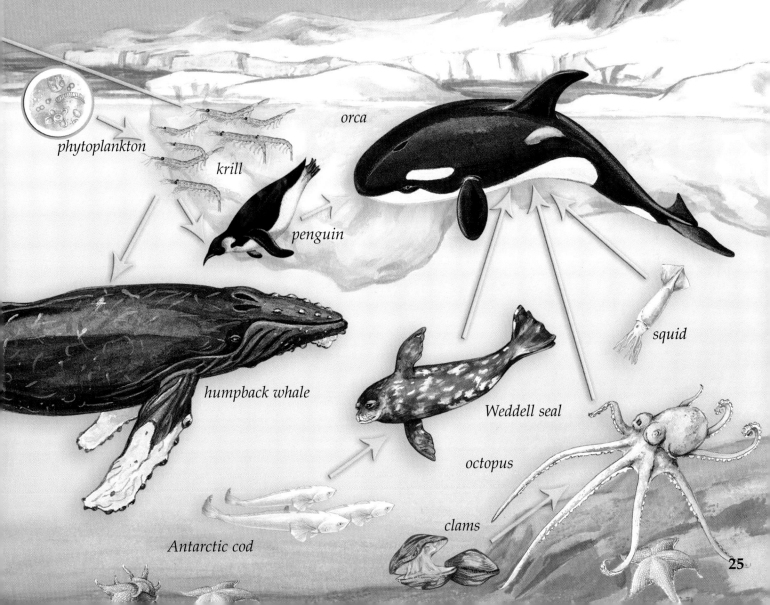

phytoplankton

krill

orca

penguin

humpback whale

Weddell seal

squid

octopus

clams

Antarctic cod

25

The polar oceans may seem isolated, but they are closely connected to the rest of the world. They affect weather and temperatures in every part of the planet. Water from polar oceans **circulates**, or travels through, every other ocean. The cold polar water helps keep temperatures in warm areas from becoming too hot for the survival of living things.

Global warming

When people burn **fossil fuels** such as coal, oil, and gasoline, they increase the amount of carbon dioxide in the air. High levels of carbon dioxide cause **global warming**, or the increase of the Earth's average temperature. Carbon dioxide is a **greenhouse gas**—it traps the sun's heat against the Earth and makes temperatures rise. The phytoplankton at the surface of the polar oceans absorb carbon dioxide to make food. By absorbing carbon dioxide, phytoplankton help reduce the amount of carbon dioxide in the air. However, there is now more carbon dioxide being produced than ever before. The temperatures of the polar oceans rise, causing fewer phytoplankton to bloom.

Sea ice helps keep the planet from overheating. It reflects sunlight back into space before its heat can be absorbed.

Rising sea levels

Scientists believe that global warming not only raises the temperature of the oceans, but also melts the ice sheets and glaciers at the poles. The loss of this ice, which normally does not melt, is a threat to polar regions and the rest of the world. Melting polar ice raises sea levels above normal around the world. The low coastal areas that are home to most of the world's population could be flooded, and the homes of millions of people and animals destroyed.

On thin ice

Global warming also causes sea ice to melt more quickly than it normally would. As more sea ice melts each summer, less multi-year ice forms each winter. Many animals, including seals, penguins, and polar bears, depend on the thick ice as a place to rest, breed, and hunt. If sea ice is too thin or melts too quickly, the populations of these animals may shrink. The loss of this ice will also cause the temperatures of the oceans to rise.

Polar bears often hunt for seals on the Arctic Ocean's sea ice. If the sea ice is too thin or melts too quickly, the bears will have fewer places to hunt. They may find it difficult to find enough food.

Threats to polar oceans

The Arctic and Southern Oceans are threatened by the activities of people, as all oceans are. People dump chemicals into the water and release pollution into the air. Often, these activities happen hundreds or even thousands of miles from the poles, but chemicals and pollution eventually find their way to the polar oceans.

Winds blow air pollution, and circulating ocean water carries water pollution to the poles. The chemicals and pollution weaken the ocean's plants and animals. Many animals get sick, and some die. Some plant and animal species are now in danger of becoming **extinct**, or no longer alive on Earth.

Tearing apart food webs

Many pollutants, including sewage and chemicals such as bleach and **pesticides**, end up in the polar oceans. Phytoplankton absorb these pollutants. When animals such as fish, squids, and krill eat the plankton, they also eat the pollutants. These animals then get eaten by whales, birds, seals, and polar bears, and the pollutants get passed along the food web. Pollutants cause many animals to become sick and even to die.

Disappearing ozone

Dangerous chemicals such as **chlorofluorocarbons** (CFCs) have destroyed the ozone layer above the polar regions. The ozone layer acts as a shield around the planet. It protects the Earth's surface from many of the sun's harmful **ultraviolet** (UV) rays. An increase in UV rays can upset the balance in the polar oceans. In the Southern Ocean, increased UV rays seem to be killing phytoplankton and krill populations. Without plankton, polar animals could starve.

Oil spills often wash up along polar coastlines, harming the shorebirds that hunt there. Oil spills are harmful to both polar oceans because oil breaks down much more slowly in cold water than it does in warm water.

If krill and phytoplankton populations are damaged, many animals further up the food chain, including the puffins above, may starve.

Protecting polar oceans

Polar oceans are difficult to explore because of the ice and extremely cold temperatures. Still, scientists spend weeks or months at a time at the poles to learn more about them. Both Antarctica and the Arctic have research centers in which scientists live and work. The scientists study the animals and plants in ocean food webs. Scuba divers brave the chilly waters in order to learn about the ocean animals.

Research in the Arctic

The International Arctic Research Center (IARC) is a place where scientists from around the world study the greenhouse effect in the Arctic region. They also study how changes in Arctic climate affect the entire climate of Earth. With this information, scientists can learn how to protect the poles, the polar oceans, and Earth's atmosphere in the future.

The Antarctic Treaty

In the past, people had little concern for the poles. They thought of Antarctica as a wasteland because no one lived there. As people learned more about the poles, polar oceans, and their important role in the health of the planet, however, they began working to protect both areas. In 1959, twelve governments from around the world signed the Antarctic Treaty. This agreement guarantees that the continent of Antarctica will be used for peaceful and scientific purposes only. The treaty also protects the animals in the Antarctic. In 1991, governments altered the treaty and added some new rules. The new agreement is called the Protocol to the Antarctic Treaty. It includes new measures to protect Antarctica and its ocean, such as a complete ban on mining for fifty years.

*Marine mammals such as walruses and seals are a source of food and clothing for the **Inuit** peoples of the Arctic. The Inuit are allowed to hunt a certain number of animals every year.*

Adult harp seals and harp seal pups were hunted nearly to extinction in the past, but today they are protected.

You can help!

Reducing pollution and global warming are just two ways to help polar oceans. You can burn less fossil fuel by reducing car travel. You can also learn about endangered polar animals that need protection. Check out these websites to learn more about polar oceans, polar animals, and polar ice:

- http://www.antarctica.ac.uk/About_Antarctica/Wildlife/index.html
- http://www.polarbearsalive.org/facts4.htm
- http://www.arctic.noaa.gov/education.html
- http://earthobservatory.nasa.gov/cgi-bin/texis/webinator/printall?/Library/PolarIce

Glossary

Note: Boldfaced words that are defined in the book may not appear in the glossary.

chlorofluorocarbons Gases found in refrigerators and spray cans, which destroy the ozone layer

climate The long-term weather conditions in an area, including temperature, rainfall, and wind

current A flow of water in an ocean that moves continuously in a certain direction

food chain The pattern of eating and being eaten

food web Two or more connecting food chains

fossil fuel A type of energy formed from the bodies of plants and animals that died millions of years ago

habitat The natural home of a plant or animal

iceberg A massive piece of ice that has broken away from a glacier or ice shelf

Inuit A group of Native people that lives in northern Canada and Greenland

mammal A warm-blooded animal that has a backbone, is covered with hair or fur, and gives birth to live young

migrate To make a long journey in order to reproduce or find food

pesticide A chemical used to kill insects

phytoplankton Tiny plants that live in water

plankton Tiny plants and animals that live in water and cannot be seen without a microscope or magnifying glass

polynya An area of open water surrounded by sea ice

predator An animal that hunts and eats others

prey An animal that is hunted and eaten by other animals

salt water Water that contains salt

tide The daily rise and fall of oceans based on gravity

Index

1 2 3 4 5 6 7 8 9 0 Printed in the U.S.A. 2 1 0 9 8 7 6 5 4 3